All about Love

Charlene Perkins

BookLeaf
Publishing

India | USA | UK

Presentation by *BookLeaf Publishing*

Web: www.bookleafpub.com

E-mail: info@bookleafpub.com

ISBN: 9789357448178

First edition 2022

To the women I love and those that love me in return. You taught me to walk with my head held high, no matter the breaking.

ACKNOWLEDGEMENT

To my mother and to my friends, I would not have survived without you.

Her to You

Lightbulb girl
sees you,
explodes, out of her glass shell;
blasts in
to your entire room.
Blinding,
for a moment,
may come off
a little too much.
Protect your eyes,
your ears
from the glare,
all that talking,
I mean energy.
Bouncing in it.
Careful!
She still believes in humanity.
Wants to see you glow.
Yes. Grow.
You may wonder,
love,
you?
Yes.
Ain't trying to get you naked,
Wants to unwrap you.
Get

deeper
under the skin
settle in
to your dark spaces.
Find what you keep hiding,
Yourself?
Your world.
She wants
to meet
to love.
She's done the mathematics.
Answers exponential
Rips away at
her heart.
Still has more to give.
Learned skill. This love,
takes actions.
Stumbled over more often than gets right.
Practicing novice
this woman of yours.
Efforts blown up in her chest,
third degree burns.
That's ok.
House of laughter, that one.
Bounce back stuff.
Don't mistake her
for the child
in her face.
Older than her eyes will tell.

Practiced melody,
her laughter.
Sweeter for the salt in it.
Taught how to heal.
Learned unbroken.
Ok to come undone.
Falls
when
necessary.
Nanny's daughter, survivor in the blood.
Birthday in the sugar cane fields.
Woman.
Loves you, always.
Loves you, bloody.
Loves you
Forever.

The narcissist—a definition

The narcissist, devoid of any ability to understand emotions or empathy, traps their conquests through mirroring. Before the discard,

they will revisit every echoed light to rob it of its color. Their prey will wonder what happened. How could anyone hurt anyone so completely? They will lose their value; forget their radiance and truly believe themselves a walking void all along.

The Women Speak

When you finally woke up, looked around, took
stock of where you had grown into.
You no longer recognized the woman residing in
your body.
How had she lost herself so thoroughly at his
feet?
Responsibility.
You kept trying to hoard it all for yourself.
We will not allow it.
You do not get to pick up where he left off.
We are here now.
We remember our history even as you slip away.
Sit now, while we share our stories.
Cupid was always a weaponized boy god.
We loved enough to fight anyway,
Knowing some battles worth the risk.
These things we endure will not keep breaking
us.
Wrought of too strong a metal;
ocean hearts and iron spines.
Maroon descendant, daughter of Nanny
elasticity in you woman.
We come from a bounce back people.
Take yourself back,
even if it means starting over from the
beginning.

Inner child,
Dandelion girl,
Your bones shook. Your voice knows its name.
We have found you.
You will grow new.
Stronger,
for having gone through it all.

Rambles, A Protest

A home is not a place.

When you can't stand I will lay down next to
you,
Together, we will knit worlds out of clouds.

These days, I wonder if it is easier to dismiss our
joyful friends. To hurt them without guilt. To
assume them the dumbest of us all for not seeing
the world for the burning morbid place it has
become. Those friends, our happy, joy to the
brim friends, though we call them blind, choose
to see every day from the angle most filled with
life.

A home is not a place. It is every person that
causes the heart to long for that place.

My bones know exactly where they came from.

I have this dancing tongue, an amalgamation of
all the women I have been.

I wear my hair big and curly, a shout in a quiet
place. It demands attention.

When I started to wear my hair curly, it grew big. Took up space I did not think I could inhabit. I had to learn to stand out instead of disappearing.

My mother has a story of personal triumph for every painful experience I bring her. In sharing them, she offers a story of survival for all the broken parts of me.

Now let me tell you about my people. We are of Earth and Sun. We survive so we can live. We dance and sing. We are a celebration in life and in death.

This land is my land, here, we grow strong women.

Let me tell you about the women from my home. They are the daughters of the maroon queen. A woman so powerful they made a myth of her sacrifice. She protected a whole country with the curve of her rear. In doing so, she saved an entire people.

If you want to know how to grow a powerful woman. Plant her in the island earth and give her space. She will take it from there.

Let me tell you about the women on the island
of my birth. They are still there; they grow and
thrive.

They are a living for a living circle of women.

Let me tell you about my mother. She is a
'scream in the hallways' kind of woman. She is
a 'chastise the gunman' kind of woman. 'He will
apologize' kind of woman. 'Let the children see
how a strong woman breaks' kind of woman.
So, they will know how to walk again with joy
in their hearts and a song between their lips.

My people are a broken island, reaching for the
sun. They will burn themselves. They will burn
each other but let any beyond our shores attack
just one and watch a whole country stand for
one.

The most sinister thing about colorism is how it
mobilizes people against themselves. Colorism
demands we fight our own bodies. None that
participates escape without scarring.
My people are a multicolored people.

Once I wanted to be as dark skinned as Nanny,
my first hero. Eventually, I learned to love the
body that grew from the island she fought for.

Her children are one out of many people. One
family, a hundred different beautiful shades.

If someone needs you broken to feel whole, run.
They will break you over and over in search for
something they can never find in another human
being then demand you take responsibility for
that failure.

I will not give my health to save you. I will not
castrate my voice to make you comfortable

The last time

It happened slowly.
The last time,
The storm creeped in
An insidious quiet rage.
It tore its way through the
Whole body.
But no one called it violent
because they could not see the damage.
It did not bloom to the surface,
a malady to point to
its own name.
It brought a flood.
The kind my mother demanded
we girls shored ourselves against
until after she died.
The earthquake that followed shook me loose
of my sanity
and removed from the beneath them
the legs of many onlookers.

It brought the breaking.
I could not hear my cries over my cries,
did not recognize my voice screaming for itself,
only the thunder swearing down off the tongue
of a small god in whose image I had renamed
myself

in fear of him, his white knuckled fists and
unknowing eyes.
When the storm settled, my world laid her body
down,
an undone desolate place, as far as the mind
could see,
certain, she would never again grow wild
through the meadows
and yet,
in only a short shifting of the sands,
new life,

A bud of yellow warmth pushes itself up out of
the scarred earth.
Head raised towards the sun, excited, for whom
she would become.

Ink

When the poems came back, they rushed. A race
to the page.
In the end, there were three or four entangled in
each other like the cords of your old
headphones. I would have to undo the knot in
order to listen to the music.

They woke me in the middle of the night,
Demanding attention.
So I wrote.
The page grew into a monster of a thing.
Nothing made sense, except the page, except the
ink, except sometimes the exercise simply to
exercise.
This is a muscle after all, that we are building,
we must fine-tune the skill in ink.

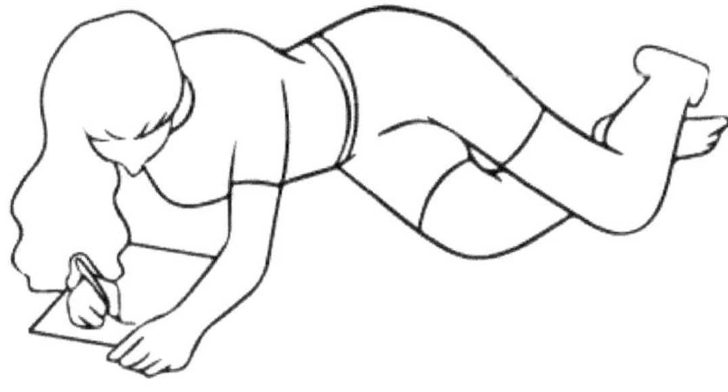

Bravery

My bravery has tears mixed in, but I'm learning
how to live the way I fall.
I've been hiding my shaking hands for too long.
I've been told a thousand times where the
weakness lies.
My courage knows what it takes to rise.

My Bravery has tears mixed in.
My Vulnerability births my greatest strength.
I've got shaking legs and hands that tremble.
My perfection, good only for a stall.

Where

Most days I live here.
On others, I wander, lost in the past trying to
find the first explosion.
It breaks but does not bleed.
It dies and no one sees.
This should look like a massacre.
Black eyes and ripped sinew.
Then no one would ask for proof of violence.
Then I would not ask.

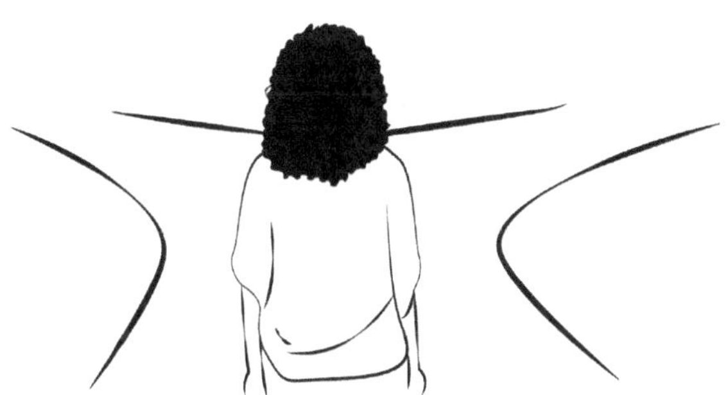

I Pledge Allegiance

I pledge allegiance to the body.
This sack of blood and bones.
Let it grow, let it jiggle and sway.
I give myself to the dream,
that unending state of possibility.
To the women I will become,
before they are no one at all.

I pledge allegiance to the hold,
to the state,
no matter the voices,
no matter the pain.

I pledge allegiance to the process,
the list and lists and breaths,
the slow inhale and slower exhale.

I pledge allegiance to the chance,
to change.
Let the gray matter godumb.
Let it wallow and soften.
Let it learn to run, let go.
Let it laugh.
Let it be.

On Love

This process of falling,
I never seem to stick the landing,
crashing.

Broken bones at the bottom of the well,
drowning, beneath all our possibilities.

And I am in trouble,
in the best way possible. Maybe.
I think.

This heart of mine,
it's big, but squishy,
soft, I mean,
with a bounce back feature, sure
but that takes... time.

Phantom Limb

My love's a phantom limb.
I wake and reach for him.
Tracing my cheeks for his fingertips
I sit spectator as the body searches and reacts to
hands and lips long ago removed.

It is a dirty trick the body plays
and all that remembering
It knows better than the heart and mind how well
the flames scar
And still, holds out for the pain.

In the heat of the flames,
the brain watches on and screams behind a
caged tongue.

The brain does not know what was lost or stolen
or given away
knows only the warning, the burning.
It remembers only the heat and the pain of
getting too close
to temporary things.
The body does not care.
The body only feels.
It wants only touch.
It reaches for its love

over and over again.
And I am held down and consumed under this
flame.

Immigrant Magic

They will tell you to pull yourself up by the
bootstraps.
You leave that for the people with shoes.
Come I will teach you how to sew. And out of a
land of watermelons, sweet peppers and thyme
we flew to a land that claimed my island. There
we gathered the crumbs from the queens table.
When they called me, outsider, we tamed our
tongues, sewed ourselves the right uniform and
continued the performance.

Come look behind the curtain, a pile of bones
on the floor. That is my brother. I heard his
insides crack the day he learned what it meant to
live in his skin and dress the way he wants to.
Give him time he will wear what makes him
comfortable, but he will do it in a body made of
steel.

I have seen magic. It works at Starbucks and
builds homes in a faraway land. How do you
make so little a rope stretch far enough to pull
people out of their circumstances?

The immigrant knows that magic and she will
tell you about the prayer in the pot but you
season it with sweat.

My grandmother knew this truth the day she
found nothing but Salvation Army flour in the
kitchen she said gather the rain and with the
movements of these hands we will have manna
tonight.

Do you know that one, they split the woman in
two and she lives?
We know that trick. We perform it every time we
say home and must differentiate which one.

So when I say this field is like magic, I mean
look, nothing in my hands nothing up my
sleeves now stand back. I'm about to amaze you.

Ink

It's been six months, six days, since the last
words slipped from my fingertips and bled an
inkling all over my page. I can hear the poems
leaving, falling into a canyon of what could have
been.
I am further and further away from the woman I
thought I would one day become.
I am drowning in the alienation of it. Feels like
losing myself.
I am losing her.

Mommy

Mommy comes home and talks about the shit at
work.
That's not a euphemism.
She is up to her elbows in it.
Tells me never to turn my nose up at the ass that
feeds it.

Actually, my mother has a soft tongue and an
iron heart.
She does not swear for fear of hurting someone
else.
An act of respect she practices even in private.

Mommy loves like the ocean, always giving
back;
As open as the clear blue sky.
She will also wreck the ground beneath your feet
for wrongdoing,
Especially at the expense of someone she loves.
I have never met a person my mother could not
love.

Steve

What I should have said when you had to leave.
Steve. My darling, bastard.
I found myself in turmoil as disbelief mangled
itself from chest to spine,
The paralysis, efficiently medieval.
While you wrenched the largest chunk of frozen
peanut butter from the cold embrace of its
chocolate ice-cream protector.
In my house, with my spoon, rage seems
inadequate a descriptor.

But I'm getting a little behind of myself
I meant to say, sorry, for the things I said and
wrote and sent when the hurt screamed so loud, I
could not hear my own grace.
I'm not talking about dessert anymore. The
leaving.
When you said your boundaries down in the
name of mental health had I given charge to my
empathy I would have responded, "Please don't
go. This hurts too much. I had not hoped for a
partner, still don't, I made preparations for a
temporary, most likely prolonged departure, but
I shatter and drown in the required permanence
you speak of.

I had let grow the idea of companionship and
fear the devastation in uprooting it now."
When you reiterated your decision, grounded in
a crooked certainty and human accountability. I
would have shored up my tongue even as the
damn broke against my tears.
I feel too much, to avoid getting washed away.
I am sorry. Even in my recreations I cannot spare
you the rain.
Thank you for the courage of your truth, for the
respect it took to listen as I thrashed and
sputtered in search of a branch to hold.

Had I known how to swim, I would have told
you, I admired your strength.
I took notes on the 'how' you modeled in
quieting the heart on the journey to better.
I hope you never let anyone hand you shame for
the paths you take to healthy.
I imagine you'll get it wrong often.
That there will be other's, beautiful and wild, for
them you may try a dirt road or two believing in
the timing and the weather only to walk away
with bloody hands and unwanted lesson
dandelion seeds between your teeth. I know that
failure well.
I lost my name to it.

I will truly never understand your struggle. We
all have the same destination, true, but none of
us get there the same way. Right or wrong turn,
trusting yourself seems, at least, the right
direction. I have no anger for you.
Only this. If we meet again on the other side of
well, if your boundaries no longer need such
sturdy walls. I offer you time,an extra spoon,
peanut butter and frozen chocolate embraces.
You
bring the soil. I'll supply the rain. We can scatter
the seeds pulled from the fruits of the lessons
learned on the way.

Faithful empathy and honesty often feel sadistic.
Like we drank out hearts numb, drove drunk into
the night, a planned crash into the trusting arms
of someone that chose to love us so we could
glee at the wreckage, pull a tale worth a spin into
the ears of anyone willing to listen.
I trust you with hard truths. I died once for a lie.
I will not do that again, instead.
I will train my courage on the bitter taste of
honesty, even as it cuts deep. Let not this cup be
taken from me. I have seventy-seven times a
thousand second chances pouring from my
bleeding heart.
I can spare a few for you.

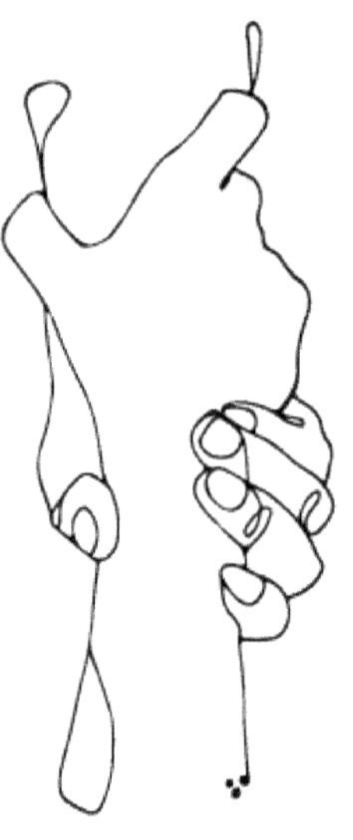

On Learning to Love Again

After the end of the world,
I braced for the emptiness.
I thought, as everything burned, that nothing else
would grow.
I waited for the memories to grind me down.
I thought loneliness would sweep me away.
I waited.

But as the smoke cleared and the ash fell, you
came.
Brought cover, watched the sky rain.
You did not speak.
Just made your presence known.

Alone
At the end of the world I wasn't alone.
When the ground, scared, after all that dying, sat
empty as far as the eyes could see.
You cried with me.
Gave permission for the rain.
Held the body as it shook itself open.
You brought bread, broke it and ate with me.
When the waters receded, small buds of joy
poked their heads above the soil.
A reminder that life held on here.

I did not have to fight.
You, my silent army, formed a defense barrier so
I could break.
You told the loneliness if it wanted me,
it would have to go through you first.
Every, are you OK?
What do you need?
Every, what time will you be there?
You can always come over.
I have an extra room, space on the couch,
we made spaghetti, want to share, wanna share?
Do you need a bed?
Do you have enough?
Do you have enough?
You were enough
and that,
that is love.
That is love.

Nanny

They shot Nanny in the ass and I wonder
sometimes.
Was she protecting her children, arms
outstretched to the wind,
catching every stray shot,
so, someone else would not have to?
Or scouting?
Children moving swiftly on callous heels.
Did someone slip?
Did the soldiers fire wild into the darkness of the
trees?
I wonder what it takes to watch your children
stripped of their name and birthright, transported
to a foreign land and still have the courage it
takes to fight.
How many did she watch float away, tied to
each other?
A garland of dark stolen lives thrown overboard
without care.
I would ask her If I could; how?
After everything was stolen, did she walk tall
enough to lead?
I don't know what it takes to be a strong woman.
But I came from Nanny's daughter.
Iron in the blood,
lifts her colonized body off the broken red earth.

Births black girls one hundred shades lighter.
All told they had nothing to offer beyond their
hips.
All walked out of the sugarcane fields, got back
to the planting.
Teaching their babies about the world,
by refusing to let it take them.
Telling of the land they came from.
Sometimes if I listen, I think I can hear the
percussion of their song
brought over on the tongues of their mothers.

They killed Nanny.
Shot her in the back.
They didn't look her in the eyes.
But then, they never saw her coming.

Gethsemane

Today, I cried a Crimson River in Gethsemane.
Laid down by my burdens.
Broken by Judas's kiss.
How it soured the tongue,
tore the life from within.
What was it worth?
Thirty pieces of silver?
Am I to carry this cross?
Instead, I bury my feet in the ground.
The disciples unsheathe their weapons.
Ready for battle.
What worth to die so brutal a death?
Father.
Where did I leave my trust,
if not in you?
I know you are watching.
I know you have a purpose
and I will follow.
Tomorrow.

Hail Mary Club

We, the Hail Mary club,
Have dragged the virgin mother,
kicking and screaming to the emergency room
demanding
one last answered prayer.
She knows the strength it takes to scream SOS.
It's pulling her hair out
for a response,
We are a sacrilegious bunch
and desperate.

Johnny

I knew exactly who you were the first time we
met.
We talked into the silence and out of it
We were not soulmates or lovers,
We were better,
than any of them could have ever hoped to be
Two people, cut from the same cloth sent out in
different directions
So, when we found each other, and we would
find each other
There would already be an adventure under our
tongues
We could sit, piece the puzzle pieces back
together and
Watch
As they horizoned, beautiful

This... is not the picture we build
Johnny, we saw it
It looked like

Two people

Lying backbone to floorboard for weeks
When only one was incapable of moving
Being so comfortable with someone

That when they left
With the ticker in your chest
You knew it would keep on singing, even though
you just met

It looked like... like the rickshaw that kept you
dreaming
Never asking, just knowing this,
Was always worth it
Like borrowed lungs when breathing was too
painful to be done alone
Knowing you were never alone
Like magic

Johnny!
They made you a box to fit
Constructed measurements from memories
Lamenting rose trees preparing for spring
I told them, you were gone to reap a story

Yet I find myself distance making, as they do
Between this place and the next
Clutter brain, no cure
Tell me you are out there
My heart still folded neatly in your palms
Keeping perfect timing with your pulse
Your pulse, kept us dancing
When this world we call a home switched off the
speakers

Left us,
In the silence

I said you were gone to harvest a story
One we planted as children
But Rachel refuses to be comforted
Tells me, this life is no lullaby
And I was no baby needing to hear it.

I do not hear her.
I am somewhere on the coast of Jamaica
Pressed against your chest
Lost between your elbows
Our synchronized heartbeats reminding me I'm
still here
You're still here

Indigo eyes, calming like the ocean.
Do you remember why we argued?
Pointing to the waves.
Do you remember what you said?
You said, 'See the way they are constantly
returning?
To kiss the lips of the shoreline, two separate
Entities carved from to the same source
Meant for each other
We are not truly ourselves without each other'.

That night old friend, we danced

On the magic of the full moon's wings
The only music, the night and the percussion
Coming from under our skins
We never danced like that before
Or ever again
Friend, you left with the waves
I am shorelined
I am waiting…

Warnings

There is a flame and burn period.
She calls it the ADHD's got your number.
You are now her best obsession, friend.
If you survive this.
She has some theories:
One, you walk around inside a brain as crowded
as hers.
Two, you are a narcissist.
Three, you are as broken inside as she feels on
her worst days.
Well, you shimmer, whatever the case.
You may believe she has fallen in love with you.
She has a very good exclamation.
You are shiny new human and
She has fallen in love with you.
It's not that she wants to see you naked.
She wants to unwrap you.
Peel back every layer
until your humanity stands exposed and fragile.
She wants to get dirty with you,
explore your crevasses.
The you you are too ashamed to leave out in
public.

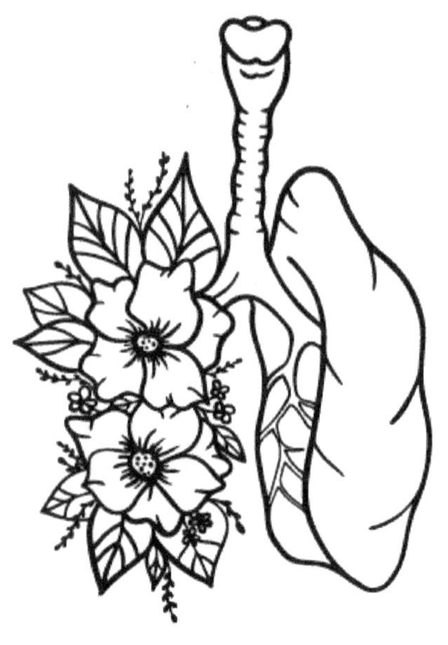

www.ingramcontent.com/pod-product-compliance
Lightning Source LLC
LaVergne TN
LVHW021256200726
843509LV00012B/1686